David

Sam Wellman

Illustrated by
Ken Landgraf

BARBOUR
PUBLISHING, INC.
Uhrichsville, Ohio

Published by Barbour Publishing, Inc., P.O. Box 719, Uhrichsville, Ohio 44683 http://www.barbourbooks.com

 **ecpa** Member of the Evangelical Christian Publishers Association

Printed in the United States of America.

David

"IS THAT A LION?"

1

"Is that a lion?" blurted out young David.

He stopped strumming the small, nine-stringed harp he propped in his lap. Did he see a tawny form creeping from a ravine near his flock of sheep? He stood up. No, it was not a lion but a stray dog. He clapped his hands and the dog bolted back up the ravine.

David's heart was beating hard. He trusted God, or thought he did. But was that trust great enough to allow him to face a lion? He picked up his harp and sang a psalm, an old sacred song that his father Jesse had taught him. It was said among the Jews the great Moses had written it. It began:

> *Lord, you have been our dwelling place*
> *throughout all generations.*
> *Before the mountains were born*
> *or you brought forth the earth and the world,*
> *from everlasting to everlasting you are God.*
>
> *You turn men back to dust,*
> *saying, "Return to dust, O sons of men."*
> *For a thousand years in your sight*
> *are like a day that has just gone by. . . .**

It was a long song, but David sang the whole thing. He was very good at remembering the exact words of songs, as well as the words of the five sacred books of Moses.

---

*Psalm 90:1–4

DAVID SANG THE PSALM.

DAVID

The life of a shepherd boy could be lonely. Wise boys used their time alone in the fields to grow stronger. David was fifteen, and he made the most of being by himself. He prayed to Almighty God, often composing his prayers as poetry. Then he sang his prayers while he strummed the strings on his harp.

Apparently he played well. When he was allowed to join his family in Bethlehem, even his older brothers listened to him. Usually they didn't want to hear what he had to say and told him to be quiet. But David's oldest brother, Eliab, and two more of his seven brothers were soldiers in King Saul's army, so they were rarely at home anyway.

"But they are at home now," reflected David.

He wished he was there, but the sheep had to be tended. He rose and stowed his precious harp inside the small hut he slept in. It was covered by heavy mats of goat hair, woven by the women of his family. The grass-carpeted hills where David

THE LIFE OF A SHEPHERD BOY COULD BE LONELY.

shepherded his father's sheep were rocky with scrubby bushes.

Like all shepherds, David carried a staff and a heavy club called a rod. He used the staff to prod stubborn sheep, although most came willingly to his call. His heavy club was used to strike unwelcome intruders. Usually, though, the intruders—like wolves or hyenas—were too far away to hit with a club. Then he had to drive them away with a well-placed shot from his sling. He practiced using his sling as much as he did his harp.

"It is a well-known sacred story that among the ancient Jewish armies there were seven hundred Benjamites who could sling a stone at a hair and not miss," David reminded himself (Judges 20:16). "But many have forgotten how deadly this skill is."

David belonged to the tribe of Judah—one of the twelve Jewish tribes descended from the patriarchs Abraham, Isaac, and Jacob. Jacob lived about one thousand years before David. Moses, the

HE PRACTICED USING HIS SLING.

great Jewish prophet who took the Jewish tribes out of slavery in Egypt, lived about five hundred years before David.

The Benjamites, the Jewish tribe famous for their skill with slingshots, were neighbors to David's tribe of Judah. King Saul was a Benjamite. He had united many of the Jewish tribes. Many people thought of him as the first Jewish king. That was why David's older brothers fought for him.

"There is another reason I practice with my sling," he murmured as he selected some rounded, egg-sized rocks. "The day may come when an intruder will not run away."

David could scarcely bring himself to think of what that would be like. Every once in a while, his father and his brothers had warned him, a lion wandered up from the valley of the Jordan River far to the east. David had seen a dead lion once. It had been old, desperate for easy prey. David couldn't imagine facing such a huge beast—old or

DAVID HAD SEEN A DEAD LION ONCE.

young—with such enormous daggers for claws and ferocious spikes for teeth.

Large brown bears lived in the rocky recesses of these highlands. Bears, too, were known to try to take a sheep from time to time. Yes, some day David might have to fight such terrors as these—all alone with nothing but his club and a sling. So he had a very good reason to practice with his sling.

As he hurled rocks with such speed that they hummed through the air, he thought of another song:

They have tracked me down,
they now surround me,
with eyes alert, to throw me to the ground.
They are like a lion hungry for prey,
like a great lion crouching in cover. *

But why stop his poem at the danger? Why not

*Psalm 17:11–12

LARGE BROWN BEARS LIVED IN THE HIGHLANDS.

appeal to God, whom David loved so much?

> *Rise up, O LORD, confront them,*
> *bring them down;*
> *rescue me from the wicked by your sword.**

Jewish poetry did not rhyme; it was written in couplets or pairs of lines. The second line usually used different words to repeat the thought in the first line. David had composed thousands of couplets in his days as a shepherd.

"David!" boomed a voice in the air. A man walked across the grassy slope. He was dressed like David, with a long heavy cloak flapping over a simple light tunic. Of course his clothes were made of wool. Except for leather sandals, would the sons of Jesse wear anything but wool? It was one of David's brothers. David's brother yelled, "You must go home right away. Father wants you!"

"But what of the sheep?"

---

*Psalm 17:13

"DAVID!" BOOMED A VOICE.

DAVID

"I'm to watch them until you return."

"But why am I being called?"

"Just obey!" snapped the brother. "Go! Run, little brother!"

David loped across the hillsides. Was someone sick at home? His father, Jesse, wasn't sick, was he? Maybe not. David's brother said it was his father who wanted him. Still, David's father was no longer young. Nor was David's mother. Perhaps she was sick. After all, she had given birth to more than ten children.

David's heart pounded as he saw the walled town of Bethlehem in the distance. Outside the walls lived most of the men who ran large flocks of sheep and goats. Some lived in sturdy goat-hair tents; some lived in simple mud-brick houses. David steeled himself and walked onto his father's property.

"God, let this problem be small," he prayed.

Outside Jesse's drab brick house was a bouquet of color from many large tents draped with

DAVID SAW THE WALLED TOWN OF BETHLEHEM IN THE DISTANCE.

dyed hides. The floors of the tents were covered with elegant floral carpets. A big crowd of people, including all the elders, were gathered there.

David's heart sang when he saw his father sitting by the main residence. Jesse seemed in full health. And there was his mother standing with David's sisters. Praise God she was all right. Now David saw that a calf was being sacrificed to God. A man David didn't know was seated with his father and the elders. The stranger looked to be about eighty years old. His robe was as fine as any David had ever seen.

The old man rose suddenly. "So this is the one!" he cried in surprise, looking up as if speaking to no one but God. He directed his attention to David. "You are indeed a handsome young fellow. Strong and healthy-looking."

"God be with you, sir," answered David, bowing.

"Kneel," said the old man. "I am to anoint you."

David saw the old man take a horn encased on both ends by bright yellow metal. The metal seemed

"SO THIS IS THE ONE!"

too bright, too yellow for brass. Could it be gold? The old man poured oil from the horn into his hand.

David inhaled the oil's sharp, spicy fragrances. Many fragrances were in the fine oil. Was that myrrh he smelled? Some delicious scents he could not identify. Was one the famous spikenard? Who was this very important old man? David felt the warm oil soak into his hair. The old man's gentle hands spread it over his head.

Suddenly David no longer wondered about what was happening. The Holy Spirit entered him. Never had David felt so fearless and so full of peace.

The old man left abruptly. Then David got up.

"Who was he?" David asked his father.

Father Jesse seemed in shock. "He said he was Samuel from Ramah."

"The great prophet Samuel!" gasped all the brothers at the same time.

THE HOLY SPIRIT ENTERED HIM.

"I ALSO SAW SAMUEL ONCE."

2

"Yes, he said he was Samuel," said one of the elders.

"I saw Samuel years ago," said another elder. "That old man didn't look like Samuel to me."

"I also saw Samuel once," said another. "I believe the old man was Samuel."

"But why was he here?" asked the oldest brother Eliab.

"I don't know," answered Jesse.

"Perhaps to anoint a king," gasped one of the elders.

DAVID

"Nonsense!" said Eliab angrily. "Samuel has already anointed a king. Saul is our king. I'll bet the old man was an imposter."

"He didn't look like an imposter," said David.

"Oh, be quiet," snarled Eliab. "Go back to your sheep, you pup."

His father gave David a puzzled look. "Yes, son, it is best that you return to the flock."

So David returned to the sheep without telling anyone the glorious feeling he had as the rich oil was put on his head. Was it truly the Spirit of God Who had entered him? David believed that it was. He also believed God did everything for a purpose. Did David's anointing somehow mean he would soon be put to a test?

"Whatever happens, I will trust the Lord," he promised.

In the winter, the sheep were brought down from the heights to graze very close to Bethlehem. But summer had not reached its peak yet, so David gradually worked the sheep higher into the hills.

DAVID RETURNED TO THE SHEEP.

DAVID

Some of the wild creatures in the hot lowlands sought the coolness of the heights, too. Hyenas, wolves, and bears roamed the hills, so David was always on the alert. His flock was full of young lambs. A shepherd had to defend every sheep, every lamb, just as Almighty God—the Great Shepherd—defended His people.

David put that thought into a new song:

The LORD is my strength and my shield;
my heart trusts in him, and I am helped.
My heart leaps for joy and I will give
thanks to him in song.

The LORD is the strength of his people,
a fortress of salvation for his anointed one.
Save your people and bless your inheritance;
*be their shepherd and carry them forever.**

One day, as David made his rounds of the sheep,

---

*Psalm 28:7–9

DAVID WAS ALERT.

he heard a low rumble. It was the most horrible sound he had ever heard. It was as if the very earth were growling as it supposedly did in earthquakes. Yet this awful sound was not from the rocks. David had never heard the sound before, but he knew what it came from.

"A lion," he gulped.

David gently placed his staff and heavy cloak on the grassy slope. He unslung his weighty club. The club was made from oak. It had a knot on the end as hard as iron. But it had never been called on to do what it might have to do this day.

David crouched down and crept toward the blood-chilling sound. Yes, there was the source. Not fifty yards away in a dry ravine stood a great male lion with a mane as black as a tomb! The lion had its paw on a lamb. The sound the lion had made was not a warning. It was a rumbling of pleasure. For the lion was absorbed in its tiny victim. The lamb bleated. The poor little creature was still alive. It cried for its shepherd David's mercy.

THE POOR LITTLE CREATURE WAS STILL ALIVE.

DAVID

"God, in Your great mercy, grant me strength," prayed David.

David felt power explode inside himself. He burst toward the lion. Never had he run so fast. The lion still had not seen him. David leaped the last dozen feet, swinging the club as he flew through the air. As he landed in the sand of the ravine, he brought the club down with all his might. The lion's skull whomped like a great melon. The lion snarled in anger and staggered away from the lamb. David saw blood on the lamb's white wool. He was angry at what the lion had done to the poor lamb.

Groggily, the lion turned on David. Its yellow eyes were glazed. David hammered the club down on its skull again. He leaped on the lion. Grabbing its thick black mane, he hammered its skull again and again with his club.

Finally the lion was dead. David saw the lamb rise and steady itself on wobbly legs. Then it stumbled off to find its mother. Soon it was skipping around her as if nothing had happened.

THE LION STILL HAD NOT SEEN HIM.

DAVID

The anger David had felt drained away. Never had David felt such anger. Had he done right? Was anger in itself a sin? No, David decided. Anger was wrong only if it led to sin.

"God allowed me to kill the lion in order to save the lamb," he said in amazement. "Praise God for His mercy and wisdom."

David's great moment had not happened at all the way he had imagined it. He had dreamed he would interrupt the lion's kill. He would clap his hands. The lion would stand and face him. Then David would hurl a stone with his sling. The stone would bury itself in the lion's skull. The lion would fall dead.

"God had a different plan," he admitted.

David did not boast of his triumph to anyone. He had killed the lion with God's help.

The next summer, David killed a vicious rogue of a brown bear. It, too, was in the process of killing a lamb. David beat the bear to death with his stout club. He knew that God helped him

DAVID KILLED A VICIOUS BROWN BEAR.

protect the sheep.

One day David got a visit from one of his brothers. The brother sighed. "You are to go back to father in Bethlehem. I'll stay with the sheep. Take your harp."

"Am I to attend religious services?" asked David.

"Just go, Little Brother. Obey."

David was used to being called home to attend services in a tent tabernacle or to be instructed in religion. The Jews in his day studied the five books of Moses: Genesis, Exodus, Leviticus, Numbers, and Deuteronomy. In these books were the Ten Commandments as well as many other laws.

Even the tabernacle and its courtyard had to be constructed exactly as described by Moses. The courtyard had to have north and south sides of one hundred cubits. A cubit was about one and a half feet, so these sides were about 150 feet long. The west and east sides of the courtyard were fifty cubits, or about seventy-five feet long. The courtyard was

ONE DAY DAVID GOT A VISIT FROM ONE OF HIS BROTHERS.

surrounded by curtains of finely twisted linen that hung from a specific number of posts with bronze bases and silver hooks. The curtains were five cubits high, or about seven and a half feet.

People entered the courtyard only on the east side. In the open courtyard was a bronze altar where offerings were burned.

"I offered a young pigeon once," remembered David.

The actual tabernacle—the place for worship and thinking about the presence of God—was 30 cubits by 10 cubits, or about 45 feet by 15 feet. The tabernacle had a wooden framework covered with linen and animal hides. One room held the seven-branched lamp stand called a menorah, the altar where incense was burned, and a table for "showbread"—one loaf from each of the twelve Jewish tribes.

Behind a veil of blue, scarlet, and purple linen embroidered with cherubim was the second room, called the Most Holy Place. It housed the Ark of

IN THE OPEN COURTYARD WAS A BRONZE ALTAR.

the Covenant, a chest that contained the five books of Moses and the actual stone tablets with the Ten Commandments.

The lid of the chest was called the Mercy Seat. On each end of the lid stood golden cherubim—angels with outstretched wings and heads bowed toward the Mercy Seat.

The Most Holy Place was entered only once a year and only by the high priest. Although Jews worshiped and brought sacrifices to many tabernacles, only one tabernacle had the actual Ark of the Covenant. David's father told him that this tabernacle was in the town of Kiriath-Jearim, about 15 miles northwest of Bethlehem.

As David hurried from the fields to Bethlehem, he wondered if he had forgotten one of the holy feast days of the Jews. But it was summer. The only feast day observed in summer was the Feast of the Harvest. At the Feast of the Harvest, special consideration was given to widows, drifters, children, servants, and the fatherless. These less-privileged

THE ONLY FEAST DAY OBSERVED IN THE SUMMER
WAS THE FEAST OF HARVEST.

Jews feasted that day. The Feast of the Harvest came at the same time as the wheat harvest. David's father had a small wheat field. So David could hardly have forgotten such an important feast day. Why did his father want to see him?

When David arrived in Bethlehem, his father, Jesse, was standing with a soldier. Jesse looked worried.

"Did something bad happen to one of my brothers?" David blurted out.

"DID SOMETHING BAD HAPPEN TO ONE OF MY BROTHERS?"

"KING SAUL IS LOOKING FOR A GOOD HARP PLAYER!"

3

Jesse said to David, "King Saul is looking for a good harp player. Your brother Eliab told him about you. You are to go to King Saul's camp with this soldier. But I want you to take gifts to the king."

So David left Bethlehem with a goat and a donkey loaded with bread and wine. King Saul lived in the Benjamite stronghold of Gibeah, about six miles north of Bethlehem. But David already knew from his older brothers' movements that King Saul was rarely there from springtime through fall. He was usually camped somewhere in the countryside, fighting neighboring nations.

All the Jews especially disliked the Philistines, a hostile people far to the west. The Philistines had mastered the art of making iron weapons. They even had great iron war chariots pulled by mighty warhorses. So only up in the rugged highlands— where the chariots were useless—did the Jews dare to oppose the Philistines.

The soldier led David to King Saul's camp in one of these rugged river valleys to the west. David was rushed to the king's oversized, luxurious tent.

"Play!" ordered King Saul.

"Hurry," urged an attendant. "The king has a ferocious headache."

King Saul was about fifty-five years old, but he towered a full head above everyone around him. He paced the carpeted floor of his tent, great purple robes flying behind him. His face would have been very handsome if pain had not distorted

THE PHILISTINES HAD MASTERED
THE ART OF MAKING IRON WEAPONS.

it so much. It seemed as if a knife were stuck in his skull.

David felt the Spirit of the Lord as he began strumming the strings of his harp. He knew just the song to sing. He smiled at King Saul as he played. Yes, David would soothe this anguished king:

We will shout for joy when you are victorious and will lift up our banners in the name of our God. May the LORD grant all your requests.

Now I know that the LORD saves his anointed; he answers him from his holy heaven with the saving power of his right hand.

Some trust in chariots and some in horses, but we trust in the name of the LORD our God.

KING SAUL SMILED AS DAVID PLAYED.

DAVID

They are brought to their knees and fall,
but we rise up and stand firm.

O LORD, save the king!
*Answer us when we call!**

Pain melted off King Saul's face until he actually returned David's smile.

"You sing like an angel," the king said. Suddenly he barked, "Enough for now! The pain is gone. You'll do."

He turned to an attendant. "Put this boy in the tent with my armor bearers. Teach him how to serve me in that way, too."

David could see King Saul did not really look at him. David was invisible to the king. Over the next weeks, David learned the story of Saul. The story really began with the great prophet Samuel. Samuel was also a judge. For hundreds of years the Jews had been ruled by judges and had tried to

---

*Psalm 20:5–9

HE ACTUALLY RETURNED DAVID'S SMILE.

live in peace with their neighboring nations. They fought only to protect themselves.

When Samuel grew old, his sons were too corrupt to become the next judges. The people demanded a king. Samuel warned them that a king would make great demands on them. A king would not only tax them but also would take their sons into his army to start wars against neighbors. The people insisted they did not care. They wanted to be part of a powerful nation. God was angry that the Jews rejected peaceful ways.

But later God told Samuel, "I have heard the call of the people. You must anoint as first king the son of the Benjamite Kish."

One day Samuel saw Saul, the son of Kish. Saul was taller and more handsome than any other man among the Jews. Sure that this young man should be king, Samuel anointed him. And indeed, the Spirit of the Lord entered Saul.

Yet Saul had great doubts. He wasn't sure that he could be a good king. When the day came that

SAMUEL ANOINTED HIM.

Samuel announced Saul was to be the first king, Saul was hiding. But Saul still became the king. Many Jews doubted him and made fun of him. Saul knew nothing about being a king. The first time the people asked him to defend them—against invading Ammonites—Saul was plowing a field with his oxen!

But the Spirit of the Lord filled Saul with courage. Saul rallied the Jews and attacked the Ammonites still sleeping in their tents. Not only were the Jews surprised that they were now victorious fighters, but all their enemies were surprised, too. Everyone knew that the Jews did not have blacksmiths who could make swords and spears. The Jews even had to buy their plows from other nations.

With his son, Jonathan, also commanding an army, King Saul was soon defending the Jewish highlands against every nation around them, even the very powerful Philistines. But Saul was a very troubled man. During a big battle, he did not obey

KING SAUL WAS SOON DEFENDING THE JEWISH HIGHLANDS.

God's instructions. Then he lied to Samuel about what he had done.

God told Samuel to tell Saul that He would find another king for the Jews. From that day on, Samuel never visited Saul again. All this happened years before the time David joined King Saul's camp to play the harp for him. By then, King Saul was often unhappy and had very bad headaches.

David often wondered about Samuel. *If Samuel were here now, I would know if he was the one who anointed me.*

Often David was allowed to return to his home in Bethlehem to help Jesse with his sheep. This usually happened when Saul was in good health. When his headaches returned, David was summoned.

One day David was told to go to Saul's camp for a different reason. He was called from his flock long before dawn. David could guess his mission when he saw his father standing by a donkey loaded with provisions.

DAVID'S FATHER WAS STANDING BY A DONKEY
LOADED WITH PROVISIONS.

DAVID

Jesse said, "Take this sack of roasted grain and ten loaves of bread to your three brothers in King Saul's camp." Jesse winked. "Give these blocks of cheese to the commander of their unit."

"But where is the camp now, sir?"

"They are in the valley of the Elah River, between the villages of Socoh and Azekah."

David quickly found the upper reaches of the Elah and trudged down the valley. The Elah flowed straight west and emptied into the Mediterranean Sea. Only one enemy would be in that valley: the Philistines.

When David reached Saul's sprawling camp on one side of the Elah, the air rang with war cries. The great armies were taking their positions. David quickly found the unit of his brothers, Eliab, Abinadab, and Shammah.

The Jewish army of King Saul faced an equally sprawling Philistine army across the valley. In the hilly uplands where the Philistines could not take their thousands of horse-drawn war chariots, the

THE AIR RANG WITH WAR CRIES.

Jews could fight them toe to toe. David had barely spoken to his three brothers when the ranks of soldiers began buzzing with alarm.

"There he is—again!" groaned one. "This disgrace to the Jews has been going on for forty days!"

David looked down in the valley. Advancing from the Philistines was one soldier and his armor bearer. The Philistine warrior wore a helmet and a great coat of scaled armor, all of golden bronze. His legs were protected by bronze plates, too. On his back was a great spear. Clutched in his hand was a gleaming sword. The armor bearer struggled to carry the warrior's shield.

"I can't believe my eyes," gasped David. "The Philistine warrior must be nine feet tall!"

"THE PHILISTINE WARRIOR MUST BE NINE FEET TALL!"

"CHOOSE ONE MAN TO COME DOWN HERE AND FIGHT ME!"

4

"He must be part of the race of giants from Gath," murmured David.

"Listen to the little know-it-all," one Jewish soldier snapped bitterly at David. The voice sounded like that of David's oldest brother, Eliab.

The valley boomed with the giant's voice. "Why do you Jewish cowards come out and line up for battle? Am I—Goliath—not a Philistine? Are you not soldiers of Saul? Choose one man to come down here and fight me!" The valley rumbled with the giant's laugh. "If your man defeats me, then we Philistines will serve Saul. But if I win, you must serve us!"

"Who will go?" wondered David aloud.

"I defy you Jewish cowards and your phony God!" taunted Goliath.

How dare the giant defy Almighty God! David waited for the champion of the Jews to walk down in the valley and face the giant Goliath. Jewish soldiers were stirring, but they weren't full of determination and anger. They were full of fear. A few even became so unnerved that they ran back up into the hills. David could not believe what he was hearing and seeing.

"You would think some poor fool would take Goliath on," grumbled one Jewish soldier. "After all, King Saul is offering his champion not only his daughter in marriage but a fortune as well."

"King Saul is offering all that?" asked David in surprise.

David's oldest brother, Eliab, became furious.

THEY WERE FULL OF FEAR.

"Be quiet. We all know how good you think you are. Why have you come here, anyway? Why don't you go back to your handful of sheep!"

"Can't I even speak?" sighed David.

But he knew why Eliab and the others were so touchy. Goliath made them all feel like cowards. And his taunting had been going on for forty days! The entire Jewish army was being disgraced. There was not one man who would face the giant for King Saul. Suddenly David knew the Spirit of God was moving him to act. He slipped away to the grand tent that was King Saul's. As he expected, King Saul was not in a good mood.

"If only I were younger!" growled Saul, "but I'm almost sixty years old now. I can't fight a giant in his prime."

"Perhaps I can help, Your Majesty," volunteered David.

"Who are you, boy?" asked King Saul, startled.

"I often play the harp for you," answered David, who knew King Saul never actually saw him.

"IF ONLY I WERE YOUNGER!" GROWLED SAUL.

"What do you want? I didn't send for you to play the harp for me. I don't have a headache, but I should!"

"No Jew should lose heart this day, Your Majesty. I will fight the Philistine."

Saul groaned. "Don't be ridiculous. You are a boy. Goliath has been a warrior for many years."

"I may seem a boy, Your Majesty, but I have killed a lion and a bear." David knew that at last it was time to tell of his success with the wild beasts.

"A lion? A bear?" Saul seemed to see David for the first time. "You are telling the truth, aren't you?"

"Just as the living God protected me from those great raging beasts, He will protect me from this giant."

"God protects you?" King Saul was excited now. "Put my armor on this champion of the Jews!" he cried.

But Saul's spirits sagged again as he saw David struggle under the weight of the king's massive armor. David could scarcely lift Saul's sword. Saul

"DON'T BE RIDICULOUS. YOU ARE A BOY."

was speechless as David removed the armor and walked out of the tent. Numbly the king followed to watch.

"Maybe David's death will make one of my real soldiers want to fight Goliath," grumbled the king.

David carried only his staff and his sling. He paused in a dry creek bed on his way down into the valley and selected five smooth, egg-sized stones. Then he continued into the valley to face the giant.

The giant smiled. At last he would be able to kill some Jewish fool. David knew he must be thinking David was an armor bearer for the Jewish champion. Eventually Goliath shrugged and frowned. Where was the Jewish soldier? Then he must have noticed the fire in David's eyes.

"What!" screamed Goliath. "Am I a dog that you cowardly Jews throw me sticks?"

"You come against me with sword and spear," cried David, "but I come against you in the name of the Almighty God!"

THE GIANT SMILED.

DAVID

"Come on then with your phony God!" yelled Goliath angrily. "I will soon throw your dead carcass to the buzzards and the jackals!"

David yelled as loud as he could, "Today I will prove the God of the Jews is real and living!"

"Enough of your silliness," growled Goliath, and he began to advance on David. He balanced the spear that he intended to hurl through David.

David, full of the Spirit of the Lord, calmly placed one of his perfect stones in the pocket of his sling. Like the Benjamites, he could hit a hair fifty feet away. Goliath was that close now. David twirled the sling until it hummed like a thousand angry hornets. He let one end of the sling go. The stone blurred straight to its target. *Whack!* Goliath blinked and toppled forward. The earth shuddered. Was he dead or just stunned?

David never knew himself—nor did anyone else—because within seconds he had dashed over to draw Goliath's own great sword from its scabbard. In spite of its enormous weight, David had

WAS HE DEAD OR JUST STUNNED?

the strength to heft it high in the air. He swung it thundering down into the giant's exposed neck.

"What is that deafening roar?" said David, looking up.

The hillsides had erupted. Both armies were screaming and moving. The Philistines had panicked and were running toward the main road to their home. The Jews fell upon them, at last fighting like true soldiers of the Almighty God.

Abner, King Saul's cousin and his greatest general, came to David. He told David to bring the severed head of Goliath to King Saul. That was the custom in those days. It proved that the enemy was truly destroyed. David could barely carry the giant's heavy head. It was displayed in King Saul's tent.

"Look!" roared King Saul. "Buried deep in the giant's forehead is David's stone!"

King Saul was delighted. His son Jonathan was especially pleased with this champion for the Jews, David from Bethlehem. His eyes seemed to

THE JEWS FELL UPON THEM.

recognize David as one of God's chosen heroes. First Jonathan put his own tunic on David, then his belt, his sword, his bow, even his robe! King Saul seemed less pleased with David with each generous gift from Jonathan.

But then Jonathan stunned everyone. "I swear my friendship to David in the name of the Lord!"

David was filled with joy. "And I swear my friendship to you in the name of the Lord!"

When Jonathan and David pledged everlasting friendship to each other as a sacred covenant with the Lord, David could see King Saul had to fight becoming angry. Saul was a very handsome man, and the slightest anger soured his face. David knew only too well that Saul could change from happiness to rage in seconds. So David left the king's presence.

The hillsides were alive with activity. After the Jewish army plundered the Philistine camp, King Saul led it back through the highlands toward Gibeah. Crowds of Jews greeted them everywhere.

THE HILLSIDES WERE ALIVE WITH ACTIVITY.

DAVID

The soldiers told them of David's heroism.

Women danced among the triumphant warriors and played music on tambourines and small
three-stringed harps called lutes. In exuberant joy
they sang over and over again:

Saul has slain his thousands,
and David his tens of thousands. *

David heard that King Saul was offended.
David was too popular in Saul's mind. Now when
Saul looked at David, the young harper was no
longer invisible. David had become an object of
suspicion, perhaps even of loathing.

"I must watch the king as carefully as he
watches me," David warned himself.

The next day David was summoned to play the
harp for King Saul. This was at King Saul's palace
in Gibeah. The large palace was fine for its day,
built not of mud bricks but of rounded cobbles

---

*1 Samuel 18:7

"SAUL HAS SLAIN HIS THOUSANDS,
AND DAVID HIS TENS OF THOUSANDS."

DAVID

carefully selected from the beds of streams. The interior of the stone fortress was softened by many beautiful drapes and carpets. King Saul and his court lounged on cushions while David strummed the harp and sang:

O LORD, our Lord,
how majestic is your name in all the earth!

You have set your glory
above the heavens.
From the lips of children and infants
you have ordained praise
because of your enemies,
to silence the foe and the avenger.

When I consider your heavens,
the work of your fingers,
the moon and the stars,
which you have set in place,
what is man that you are mindful of him,

DAVID STRUMMED HIS HARP AND SANG.

DAVID

*the son of man that you care for him?**

David noticed the king's handsome face became more and more troubled. If King Saul would only be patient, he would soon know David's song would confirm his right to rule.

"I must rid myself of this nuisance!" the king suddenly shrieked, and he threw a spear.

---

*Psalm 8:1–4

"I MUST RID MYSELF OF THIS NUISANCE!"

DAVID DODGED THE SPEAR.

5

King Saul's spear came straight at David!

David dodged that spear and a second spear. Then he dashed off through the many rooms of the palace. He would avoid King Saul until the man calmed down. Surely, reasoned David, the king was momentarily out of his head.

What happened after that seemed to prove it.

"I'm putting you in command of one thousand soldiers," said King Saul to David later, as if nothing had happened. "I want you to campaign against my enemies in the countryside."

So David took the men out in the country. He suspected King Saul thought this would expose him as a mere shepherd boy who knew nothing about soldiering. But Jonathan, who was a very experienced general, advised David on how to command. And David, who knew the Jewish highlands well—every hill, every forest, every cave—did well with his one thousand soldiers.

Rarely were he and his thousand surprised by an attack. Often they fell upon encampments of invading enemy soldiers. Although fighting put blood on David's hands, he was sure God allowed men to fight invaders of the Jews, just as surely as God allowed the shepherd to fight the predators of sheep. He and his men triumphed over many invaders.

Months later, David was summoned by King Saul. He was still hailed as a hero. Now he had even more triumphs to his name.

"You seem to have forgotten I promised my

DAVID KNEW THE JEWISH HIGHLANDS.

daughter to the victor over Goliath," said Saul, unable to disguise his dislike. "Now I offer you my daughter Michal."

"But I don't deserve to be the king's son-in-law," answered David.

King Saul didn't seem to know how to take David's refusal. Was David truly modest? Or was he slighting his daughter? The terrible-tempered, unpredictable King Saul let it pass.

Soon the king learned that his daughter Michal actually loved David. Again he offered his daughter to David. How could David refuse now?

But Jonathan warned David that the king might not be doing it because he wanted to honor his daughter's wishes. David again modestly told the king he did not deserve to be his son-in-law. This time the king did not accept his refusal.

"The only price you must pay me for my treasure of a daughter is triumph over the Philistines," said King Saul.

Then the king asked David to conquer the

"I DON'T DESERVE TO BE THE KING'S SON-IN-LAW."

Philistines down in the plain. There they were virtually invincible in their chariots. David suspected that the king intended to send him to his death. But David was sure God was with him, so he did as the king asked. This time David was the invader, but he reasoned he was doing the bidding of his king. And this king had been anointed by Samuel on orders from God.

When David returned after defeating the Philistines in several battles, Saul arranged the wedding. A wedding was a great occasion, especially for a princess. Michal waited at the palace. Her face was covered with a veil, and she wore a richly embroidered white gown. Dressed in elegant robes given to him by Jonathan, David arrived, accompanied by his family and friends. His procession also included musicians, singers, and dancers.

In a short ceremony, King Saul gave his daughter Michal to David. Then the married couple left for the house David had rented in Gibeah. All the way the procession danced and celebrated.

THE WEDDING WAS A GREAT OCCASION.

DAVID

At the house the celebration continued. Guests were feasted and entertained for no less than seven days!

King Saul seemed more upset than ever. Everything always seemed to turn out in David's favor. Jonathan told David his father was now convinced God had chosen David to become the next king. Saul might never accept David as his successor. In fact, Saul might be asking men to kill David.

Jonathan urged David to go into hiding until he could find out for sure if his father planned to kill David. When Jonathan returned to David, he told him his father had assured him he was not angry at all. He even wanted David to play his harp for him again. So David played.

Once again King Saul was seized by a fit. "Take this, you upstart!" he screamed.

David ducked just in time to avoid the spear Saul threw at him. He left the palace. When he reached his own house, David was not particularly worried because King Saul's fits came and went.

GUESTS WERE FEASTED AND ENTERTAINED.

DAVID

But this time Michal, David's wife and Saul's daughter, urged him to hide.

"Men are watching the house," she cried. "They have been ordered to kill you in the morning!"

David lowered himself out a back window and escaped. Hiding in the countryside he composed a song about his narrow escape:

Deliver me from my enemies, O God;
protect me from those who rise up against me.
Deliver me from evildoers
and save me from bloodthirsty men.

See how they lie in wait for me!
Fierce men conspire against me
for no offense or sin of mine, O LORD.
I have done no wrong,
yet they are ready to attack me.
*Arise to help me; look on my plight!**

---

*Psalm 59:1–4

DAVID LOWERED HIMSELF OUT A BACK WINDOW.

DAVID

This time David went to Ramah to see the great prophet Samuel. Samuel was very old, but David recognized him as the man who had anointed him. So David knew at last that God had chosen him for some great mission. He told Samuel that King Saul was trying to kill him. Samuel told David to stay with him.

Every time men arrived from King Saul to harm David, they were changed by the Spirit of the Lord. They joined Samuel and David to sing and dance in the joy of the Lord. Finally, King Saul himself arrived. The Spirit of the Lord seized him, too. He threw away his elegant royal robes and rejoiced!

But David could not stay under Samuel's protection forever. Besides, David wanted his freedom. He went to Jonathan.

"Your father is still trying to kill me," he told Jonathan.

"Kill you? Never! My father tells me everything, and he never lies to me."

SAMUEL WAS VERY OLD.

"Perhaps once that was true. But when you pledged your loyalty to me, he has not trusted you."

Jonathan trusted David completely. "How can I help you?"

"I'm supposed to join your father at his palace in Gibeah for the feast for the New Moon. But I fear a trap. I'll hide in the area until you find out what he intends to do. Meanwhile, you can say you gave me permission to go to Bethlehem to be with my family. If he becomes extremely angry, I believe it will be because he planned to trap me."

Jonathan devised a plan to let David know what he found out about his father's intentions. David was to hide behind a boulder in a field beyond the palace. Jonathan would shoot arrows into the field and send a small boy to fetch them. If he yelled, "No, they are closer this way!" it would mean David could come into the royal court safely. But if Jonathan yelled, "No, they are farther beyond!" David must flee far beyond the royal court and the town of Gibeah.

JONATHAN DEVISED A PLAN.

DAVID

At the agreed-upon time, David hid behind the boulder.

Then he heard Jonathan's cry. "No, they are farther beyond!" Now even Jonathan knew the truth! King Saul did want to kill David. David stepped out from his hiding place and bowed in appreciation to Jonathan three times. He could see Jonathan was filled with shame over his father's sick rage. Jonathan renewed his pledge of loyalty to David.

"Go in peace," he yelled to David, "for the Lord is our Witness that we will be friends forever."

But without food or weapons or soldiers, David had never been in a more desperate situation.

HE HEARD JONATHAN'S CRY.

DAVID FLED TO THE VILLAGE OF NOB.

6

It was now clear to David that King Saul wanted him dead. David certainly could not enter the nearby fortress city of Jerusalem. It was held by the Jebusites, who were enemies of the Jews. So David fled to Nob, a village south of King Saul's Gibeah and east of Jerusalem.

Although Nob did not have the Ark of the Covenant, it had the main Jewish tabernacle and many priests. There David could seek God's guidance. David was hungry, too.

DAVID

Ahimelech, the high priest in Nob, had only show bread, the bread consecrated to God. However he allowed David to eat the bread. The high priest also gave David a sword.

In Nob, David noticed the Edomite Doeg, one of King Saul's servants. Doeg would surely go report his whereabouts to King Saul, but David did not harm him.

"I must go far away from the Jewish highlands," realized David.

His desperate flight west took him down into the coastal plain among the Philistines. Even though he was older and now wore a beard, he was recognized as the Jew who had killed Goliath of Gath. As he was dragged before the king of Gath, David heard from his captors that he would surely be killed. He was a man far too dangerous to let live.

David pretended to be crazy, barking and whinnying, letting his mouth drool onto his beard. The king of Gath was alarmed. Who knew if this

THE HIGH PRIEST GAVE DAVID A SWORD.

craziness might spread?

"Why bring him to me?" the king shouted. "Am I short of madmen? Get him out of my palace!"

David would find no refuge from King Saul among the Philistines. Now he fled to some caves near Adullam, up in the Jewish highlands. This refuge was about halfway between the main strongholds of King Saul and the Philistines. In the cave he composed songs as he always did to praise the Almighty. Part of his composition about his narrow escape in Gath said:

The righteous cry out, and the LORD
hears them; he delivers them from all
their troubles.
The LORD is close to the brokenhearted
and saves those who are crushed in spirit.

A righteous man may have many troubles,
but the LORD delivers him from them all;

IN THE CAVE HE COMPOSED SONGS.

DAVID

*he protects all his bones, not one of them
will be broken.* *

David's years as a shepherd boy in the highlands served him well now. For David had always
been a careful observer. Now he knew where to
find food in the wild. Not every animal and plant
could be eaten.

The Law of Moses was specific. No warm-
blooded, four-legged animal could be eaten unless
it had split hooves and chewed a cud. That meant
a Jew could eat only certain wild deer, antelopes,
and goats. Fortunately, David knew their favorite
places.

Edible birds were also defined under the Law
of Moses. Birds that gripped food in their claws
were as a rule forbidden. But that still allowed
David to eat partridges, doves, and waterfowl.
David also knew where these could be found.

No reptiles could be eaten, but all scaled fish

---

*Psalm 34:17–20

DAVID COULD EAT DOVES AND WATERFOWL.

were allowed. In addition, a person who knew the wilderness could find fruit, roots, locusts, and honey to eat.

"I can survive very well by myself," admitted David. "God provides."

But he missed his wife, Michal. Would he ever see her again? Soon David was joined by his father, Jesse, and his brothers. His brothers no longer regarded him as the know-it-all little brother but as a mighty warrior. They knew now that Samuel's visit to Bethlehem heralded a great destiny for David.

Over the next weeks, many men who were angry with King Saul joined David. When David had four hundred men, he took his father and mother east across the Jordan River into the lowlands of Moab. There he intended to leave them with the king of Moab, who was an enemy of King Saul. Besides that, Jesse's grandmother, Ruth, the wife of Boaz, had been a Moabite. David even considered staying in Moab himself.

MEN WHO WERE ANGRY WITH KING SAUL JOINED DAVID.

But Gad, a holy prophet traveling with David, objected.

"God wants you to go back to your Jewish highlands," insisted Gad.

So David went up into the Jewish highlands, into the forest of Hereth south of the caves of Adullam. Here he foraged a living among the bountiful game and fruits of the wild. He tried not to be discouraged, but what would ever become of him in this aimless, outlaw existence? Living off the countryside with four hundred followers was much more difficult.

One day his camp was joined by Abiathar, the son of the priest at Nob who had helped David. A terrible thing had happened. The Edomite Doeg had told King Saul about David receiving help from the high priest. The high priest—Abiathar's father—and several other priests had been murdered. The king's regular soldiers refused to do it, so Doeg had performed the terrible acts himself.

David felt miserable. Could he have prevented

ONE DAY HIS CAMP WAS JOINED BY ABIATHAR.

the tragedy? But why was he blaming himself for King Saul's sinfulness? The fact that Saul's own soldiers had refused to obey the king meant the king was losing his influence.

"I must not give up," David said. "If men have been sacrificed for me, it is because God has some purpose for me."

David welcomed Abiathar into his band. Abiathar had also escaped with his father's ephod, the special vest the high priest wore over a blue robe when he served at the altar. Two onyx stones on the shoulders of the ephod were engraved with the names of the twelve Jewish tribes. The ephod brought by Abiathar made David realize even more what he owed to God and to God's chosen people, the Jews.

David and his men always helped fellow Jews when they could. Philistines raided Keilah one summer to steal the precious wheat the people had just harvested. David prayed to God for guidance. God wanted David to help Keilah.

PHILISTINES RAIDED KEILAH.

DAVID

David rushed to Keilah with his tough warriors, now numbering six hundred. They routed the Philistines. Instead of stealing Keilah's wheat, the Philistines lost all their goods and livestock!

But David had to leave Keilah quickly. King Saul had heard what he had done and was leading his own army there to attack him. This time David did not return to the forest of Hereth but moved his camp far south into the desert of Ziph. But he did not fool everyone in King Saul's court.

"Jonathan!" cried David.

"My father searches for you night and day," Jonathan ruefully admitted. "You must find a new refuge, but God will give you the strength to prevail."

Jonathan said he knew David was destined to be king. Although many thought Jonathan would succeed King Saul, Jonathan knew David would succeed his father. Jonathan said even his father knew David was destined to be king. Why then did King Saul pursue David? Because he had

TOUGH WARRIORS ROUTED THE PHILISTINES.

separated himself from God. The prophet Samuel had seen that separation many years earlier.

"I will gladly be second to you," Jonathan promised David before he left.

Jonathan's loyalty made David's difficult life easier to bear. By the time King Saul and his army stormed into the desert of Ziph, David and his men were in the neighboring desert of Maon. But King Saul pursued him there, too. David was saved a vicious battle with the king only because Saul was called back to defend one of his towns against invading Philistines.

Meanwhile David moved his small army into the wilderness by the Dead Sea. An area there called En Gedi was full of caves. Men could live there a long time with sparkling fresh water from a spring and food from the wild goats. But if David thought he was free of Saul, he was mistaken. Soon Saul was back with his army of three thousand men, searching everywhere for David.

David and his army were hiding far back in an

SAUL WAS SEARCHING EVERYWHERE FOR DAVID.

enormous cave near the Crags of the Wild Goats. One day David could not believe his eyes. At the opening of the cave towered a man. The man peered into the inky blackness. He could not see what was in the cave. But David could see the man's crown plainly. The man was King Saul! Alone!

One of David's men whispered, "This is the day the Lord has delivered your enemy into your hands!"

"Kill him," muttered David's men.

THE MAN WAS KING SAUL!

HE CREPT UP TO KING SAUL.

7

"No, I will not kill King Saul," whispered David, "because he is the Lord's anointed."

Yet David pulled a razor-sharp knife. He crept up to King Saul, who was now gazing down into the bright sunshine of the wilderness. With the knife, David sliced a corner off the king's elegant flowing robe. Then David withdrew into the blackness until King Saul left the cave. Then he ran after him.

"My Majesty the king!" yelled David.

DAVID

King Saul whirled to face him. "David!"

"Yes. Why do you listen to those who say I am your enemy? Just now I could have killed you in the cave. But I did not. And to prove I could have killed you, I cut off the corner of your robe!" David brandished the triangle of purple fabric.

"What is that you say?" King Saul pulled up the corners of his robe. When he saw that the triangle in David's hand was indeed from the corner of his purple robe, his face clouded. This time it was not in anger but shame and remorse.

"Once again you have bested me, David. You are more righteous than I am. You treat me well, but I treat you badly."

King Saul broke down, weeping.

When the king finally regained his composure, he said, "I know you will be the future king. I wish only that you spare my descendants and that you do not wipe my name from recorded history."

"I grant you that request gladly, Your Majesty."

King Saul left, his enormous height slumped

KING SAUL BROKE DOWN, WEEPING.

in shame. But David remained with his band in the wilderness. Saul had a long history of changing his mind. David knew he could not trust the king to stay true to his word.

David was sorry to learn that the great prophet Samuel had died at Ramah. Would David ever fulfill the destiny that Samuel had promised by anointing him? It didn't seem so on some days.

"Meanwhile I and my loyal followers must survive in the wilds," he vowed.

Near Carmel lived an extremely wealthy man named Nabal. David and his soldiers had often protected Nabal's vast herds of sheep and goats from marauders. But David had never met Nabal. So he sent emissaries to negotiate a meeting. Nabal sent them away with this insulting message: "Who is this David? Many servants run away from their masters these days!"

When David heard this, he was very angry. Refusing hospitality in the countryside was a great insult. So he left two hundred of his men behind

DAVID'S SOLDIERS PROTECTED HERDS OF SHEEP AND GOATS.

with his belongings, and he marched with four hundred of his men toward Nabal's holdings. Before he could get there, he was met by a caravan. A well-dressed woman ran forward and threw herself down at David's feet.

"I am Abigail," cried the woman, "wife of Nabal. Please forgive my husband's offense against you."

Before David could answer, Abigail's servants had begun to treat him and his men to a feast. Her caravan also brought him gifts of two hundred loaves of bread, two great skins of wine, five huge sacks of roasted grain, one hundred delicious raisin cakes, and two hundred blocks of pressed figs.

Abigail told David wryly, "I pray that when you become the king of all the Jews, sir, you will not have on your conscience the slaughter of the fool Nabal and his wife, Abigail. Perhaps you will even remember your lowly friend, Abigail."

David liked Abigail very much. "Praise God

"PLEASE FORGIVE MY HUSBAND'S OFFENSE AGAINST YOU."

for sending you to me," he said. She was not only wise but beautiful, too. Nevertheless she was married. So he continued, "No, I will do nothing to your husband Nabal. Go home in peace."

But after Abigail returned to her husband, Nabal had a stroke. Nabal was much older than Abigail and ate too much food. Within ten days he was dead.

When David heard that Nabal had died, he sent a proposal of marriage to Abigail. He prayed that this very wise woman would become his wife. When she arrived several days later, his heart leaped with joy. He had lost his first wife Michal. After his escape from Gibeah several years before, King Saul had married her to another man. David had another wife named Ahinoam, whom he had married on one of his trips far to the north. Ahinoam was from Jezreel.

In those days, it was the custom of the Jewish people that if a man had enough wealth to support a large family, he could have more than one wife.

NABAL HAD A STROKE.

DAVID

But he was required to be faithful to his wives, and they to him.

One day David learned that once again King Saul was on the prowl. "He is sick in his mind again," muttered David.

This time King Saul was camped in the desert of Ziph. In the middle of the night with only Abishai, the son of David's sister Zeruiah, David sneaked into the king's huge encampment of three thousand soldiers. David recognized King Saul's oversized, luxurious tent and slipped inside. When Abishai saw King Saul lying among Abner and his other generals, he whispered to David, "Let me strike him dead."

"No," whispered David. "It is a sin to kill the Lord's anointed."

So Abishai watched in wonder as David took King Saul's spear and water jug, then slipped out of the tent. The two walked up a nearby hillside where David stood and cried out. Soon King Saul and the others stumbled groggily out of the tent.

DAVID TOOK KING SAUL'S SPEAR AND WATER JUG.

Hundreds of Saul's soldiers were now milling around.

"Who calls out?" yelled Abner.

"Abner, why didn't you guard your king?" taunted David and waved the king's spear and water jug.

"Is that you, David?" yelled the king.

"Yes, Your Majesty," answered David, "and why do you pursue me again? Did God command you to find me, or did men persuade you to search for me like a pesky flea that must be killed?"

King Saul realized that his spear in David's hand meant David once again could have killed him but had not. "Forgive my foolishness, David," he called, but he did not say why he kept following David.

Even after King Saul took his army north to Gibeah, David decided that staying in the Jewish uplands or the desert was too dangerous. For whatever reason, King Saul could never be trusted. So David went down on the coastal plain to live

SAUL TOOK HIS ARMY NORTH TO GIBEAH.

among the Philistines. King Saul would never attack David there.

Once the Philistine king became convinced David and his army would not attack him, he even gave them a town called Ziklag. The Philistine king knew David was a rebel hiding from King Saul. So he asked for David's help some day in the future when the Philistines attacked King Saul.

"You will see just what my army can do," answered David.

The Philistine king did not detect the double meaning of what David said.

"YOU WILL SEE WHAT MY ARMY CAN DO."

COULD THIS JEW BE TRUSTED TO ATTACK OTHER JEWS?

8

One year later, the Philistines marched to attack King Saul at Jezreel. David was in the rear of the army, but some of the Philistine commanders began to question the wisdom of his presence. Could this Jew be trusted to attack other Jews?

The Philistine king vouched for David, but the commanders insisted David and his army must leave. So David took his army back to Ziklag. He could not help King Saul now. Suddenly David forgot all about the fate of King Saul. As he approached his town of Ziklag, he saw that it had been attacked, plundered, and burned to the ground.

"Where are our women and children?" David asked one of the few survivors.

"They have been carried away by Amalekite raiders from the south."

David heard his men muttering against him. They were angry. Why had they gone with the Philistine king? They weren't wanted with the Philistine army anyway. In spite of his own grief, David asked Abiathar to bring him the ephod from Nob. He often wore it himself when he wanted God's guidance.

He prayed now for God's advice. God told him to pursue the raiders, so David left immediately. Far to the south they came to a deep gorge called the Besor Ravine. Two hundred of David's men were too sick to go on. So David crossed the Besor Ravine with the rest of his men. Soon they

"WHERE ARE OUR WOMEN AND CHILDREN?" DAVID ASKED.

found an Egyptian slave the Amalekite raiders had abandoned because he was too sick to travel. David nursed the slave back to health. The slave promised to take him to the village of the Amalekites.

Within days, David was returning to Ziklag. "This is now David's plunder," sang his men.

They had attacked the Amalekites and routed them. Many Amalekites escaped into the desert on camels. But David didn't care. He had his wives and children back, as well as all the other Jews taken from Ziklag. And he had a huge number of livestock and great wealth taken from the Amalekites.

When David and his army crossed the Besor Ravine, he picked up the rest of his men. The four hundred who went on the raid refused to share the Amalekite plunder with the two hundred who were too sick to continue.

But David intervened. "From this day forward, all in the army will share plunder, whether some are too sick to fight in the battle or not."

MANY AMALEKITES ESCAPED INTO THE DESERT ON CAMELS.

DAVID

When he returned to Ziklag, he decided to share the wealth with more than his army. So David sent emissaries with gifts to Bethel, Ramoth Negev, and Jattir; to Aroer, Siphmoth, Eshtemoa, and Racal; to Hormah, Bor Ashan, Athach, and Hebron; to the Jerahmeelites and the Kenites; and to people in many other places where David and his men had camped. Not all of these recipients were Jews. Abigail agreed with his generosity, sure that David would be rewarded many times over in the future.

Emissaries told each group of town elders, "David sends you gifts from the plunder of the Lord's enemies."

But just three days after David returned to Ziklag, a tattered, beaten man stumbled into town with shocking news. The man was a soldier from King Saul's army. The Philistines David had been forced to leave had virtually annihilated King Saul's army on Mount Gilboa near Jezreel. King Saul was dead. Jews to the north were fleeing their

A TATTERED MAN STUMBLED INTO TOWN.

DAVID

villages. Worst of all, David's best friend, Jonathan, was dead. If only David had been with the Philistines, surely he could have saved Jonathan!

David mourned for days. His lament began:

Your glory, O Israel,
lies slain on your heights.
How the mighty have fallen!

Tell it not in Gath, proclaim it not in the
streets of Ashkelon, lest the daughters of
the Philistines be glad.*

Oh, how he would miss King Saul, in spite of his illness, and his son Jonathan:

Saul and Jonathan—
in life they were loved and gracious,
and in death they were not parted.

---

*2 Samuel 1:19–20

DAVID MOURNED FOR DAYS.

DAVID

They were swifter than eagles,
*they were stronger than lions.**

But most of all he would miss his loyal friend:

I grieve for you, Jonathan my brother;
you were very dear to me.
Your love for me was wonderful.†

After a time of mourning, David asked God if
he should travel to the north. God told him to go
to Hebron. There David was anointed king of the
house of Judah. He also learned at Hebron that a
few Jews from Jabesh Gilead in the Jordan Valley
had managed to rescue the bodies of King Saul
and Jonathan from the wall in Beth Shan where
they had been displayed by the Philistines. In
Jabesh Gilead, the rescuers burned the bodies of
King Saul and Jonathan and buried the bones

---

*2 Samuel 1:23
†2 Samuel 1:26

THEY BURIED THE BONES UNDER A TAMARISK TREE.

under a tamarisk tree. David loved these men for keeping the bodies of Saul and Jonathan from any more humiliation.

David sent these brave men a message, "The Lord bless you for showing this kindness to your King Saul."

David learned that Abner, Saul's cousin, had survived the battle. Abner had hurriedly declared Ish Bosheth, one of Saul's surviving sons, the new king. Representatives of Ish Bosheth and David, including Abner and David's nephew Joab, met in Gibeon to discuss peace. A vicious fight broke out among several hundred soldiers. Abner killed Asahel, Joab's brother. Naturally Joab tried to kill Abner.

"Must our swords devour each other forever?" cried Abner. "Must Jews kill Jews?"

Joab learned that Abner had not started the fight. In fact, he had defended himself against Asahel only after pleading with him several times to stop. So the men put down their arms. Many

JOAB TOOK HIS MEN BACK TO HEBRON.

soldiers had been killed in the fight, and nothing had been accomplished. Joab took his men back to Hebron.

A truce of sorts was maintained, but over the years David grew stronger and the successor to King Saul grew weaker. David's own family grew strong. He had taken four more wives: Maacah, Haggith, Abital, and Eglah. Ahinoam bore Amnon, David's first son; Abigail had his second son, Kileab; Maacah had his son Absalom; Haggith had a son named Adonijah; Abital had a son named Shephatiah; and Eglah had a son named Ithream. So in Hebron, David had six wives and six sons.

In the meantime, Ish Bosheth had quarreled with Abner. So Abner negotiated with David to make David king of all the Jews. But Joab did not trust Abner and urged David to arrest Abner. David refused. He was very angry later when he learned that Joab waylaid Abner and killed him. Joab had waited years to avenge his brother Asahel's death. Even though Joab was his nephew

HE WEPT AT ABNER'S TOMB.

David was furious at his treachery. He wept at Abner's tomb at Hebron. He sang a song in his honor:

Should Abner have died as the lawless die?
Your hands were not bound,
your feet were not fettered.
*You fell as one falls before wicked men.**

The people wept too and realized David had nothing to do with Abner's murder. When Ish Bosheth heard of Abner's death, he was very frightened. His general Abner had been his main supporter. With Abner gone, Ish Bosheth's followers might turn on him. That was exactly what happened. Two brothers named Recab and Baanah killed Ish Bosheth. They brought his head all the way to Hebron to show David. But they had badly misjudged David. He ordered their execution.

With Ish Bosheth dead, all the Jewish tribes

*2 Samuel 3:33–34

DAVID ORDERED THEIR EXECUTION.

rallied around David. At thirty-seven years of age, David was finally king of all the Jews. The Philistines heard of this, too. They knew David well and decided they must crush him before he became any stronger. David learned they had sent an army after him. He and his own army beat the Philistines while they were camped at the Valley of Rephaim.

But the Philistines were not to be deterred by one defeat. They marched on David again. This time David let the Philistines attack. He commanded his troops to circle the enemy's army and attack them from behind. Once again the Philistines were beaten.

Then David went on the attack and drove the Philistines out of the Jewish highlands. He no longer commanded just six hundred men or one thousand. His army had thirty thousand men. They were well disciplined. His armies even defeated the Philistines on their own coastal plain where they were supposedly unbeatable. He

DAVID'S ARMY DROVE THE PHILISTINES OUT.

smashed them back right up to the walls of their largest cities.

"It is not my strength but God's strength that powers the Jewish army!" he cried.

Never had the Jews been so mighty. The Philistines were thoroughly beaten. David then revealed his plans for the reunited Israel.

NEVER HAD THE JEWS BEEN SO MIGHTY.

"WE MUST CONQUER JERUSALEM!"

9

To begin his plan, King David wanted Jerusalem to become the main city of his new Israel. But first David's Jewish armies had to do the impossible. They had to conquer Jerusalem. The city was bordered on the west, the south, and the east by deep valleys. Invading armies couldn't make it up the steep sides of the valleys without first being driven away.

DAVID

The north side of Jerusalem had been fortified by a huge number of trenches and other obstacles. Even the Philistines had never forced their way into Jerusalem. How could David conquer this mighty fortress?

"Jerusalem has always been able to withstand any long siege because it somehow has a supply of water," he told his army commanders.

Jerusalem was only a few miles from where David had shepherded flocks for many years. He knew natural springs of water could occur in very obscure places. Many springs were known only to a handful of people. He thought Jerusalem must have a spring like that.

"Suppose the spring is not within the city itself?" he asked.

"But that seems so unlikely," objected one of his commanders.

"Perhaps. But I command you to send scouts all around the base of the walls of the city."

JERUSALEM WAS ABLE TO WITHSTAND A LONG SIEGE.

"But they hurl stones down on people who snoop around the walls."

"Do it at night."

During this nighttime prowling, one scout found a spring below the base of the eastern wall of the city. David insisted his scout explore the spring until he knew exactly where the water went. It was that further effort that revealed the spring water was entering a tunnel that ran below the east wall of the city. David's commanders eagerly planned to block the tunnel.

David prayed a long while about the plan and then told his commanders not to do it. Instead some men must enter the tunnel and follow the path of the water. It was to his honor that many men offered to carry out this very scary task.

"It runs into a large pool below the city," explained his volunteers when they returned. "Their women lower water buckets with ropes down a shaft to gather water from the pool."

SOME OF DAVID'S MEN WOULD ENTER THE TUNNEL.

"Women do not retrieve water at night," said David. "That's when we will strike. We have all night to run a ladder up the shaft."

"Let us enter our very strongest soldiers!" said Joab eagerly. "I will gladly lead hundreds of soldiers through the tunnel and up the shaft into the heart of the city. We will have the northern gates open to the rest of our army before the people of Jerusalem discover what is happening!"

So the first moonless night, Joab led his best warriors into the water tunnel. With men that brave and that determined, the conquest of Jerusalem was simple and swift. Jerusalem became King David's city, the City of David! David terraced his new city and built a great palace out of cedars from Lebanon. He demanded that his first wife, Michal, be returned to him.

Then David had the Ark of the Covenant brought to Jerusalem. Never had he felt such joy. Wearing his ephod, he danced wildly around the

THE ARK OF THE COVENANT WAS BROUGHT TO JERUSALEM.

procession bringing the ark. Musicians filled the streets. Joy sounded from cymbals, trumpets, flutes, harps, lyres, tambourines, sistrums, and lutes.

The ark was placed in the Most Holy Place—the room of the tabernacle that David had set up according to the strict Law of Moses. Sacrifices were made to God. David also had a feast that treated everyone in Jerusalem. At the end of a wonderful day he found only one person in the city unhappy.

"How vulgar to dance around the ark like all those silly women did!" hissed Michal.

"I celebrated for the Lord. Only you feel humiliated by it," David said. At that moment, David knew Michal no longer loved him.

David was sad about Michal's coldness, but he forged ahead with his plans. He called his main prophet, who was now Nathan. David asked Nathan if it was wrong for him to live in a great cedar

SACRIFICES WERE MADE TO GOD.

palace while the Ark of the Covenant—the very seat of Almighty God—resided in a tabernacle of animal hides. He asked Nathan if there were any reason why he shouldn't build God a great temple of cedar or stone.

That night, God told Nathan to give David a message. The next day, Nathan told the king that God did not want him to build a temple of cedar or stone. David's job was to unite the Jews into a great nation. Nathan said God would give one of David's descendants the job of building the temple.

David realized how greatly God had blessed him and his descendants. "How great you are, O Sovereign LORD! There is no one like you, and there is no God but you" (2 Samuel 7:22).

Music was part of Jewish services, but David used it more than it had been in the past. Several priests of the tribe of Levi helped him build a choir of several thousand singers and musicians. The musicians played harps, lutes, and cymbals to

MUSIC WAS PART OF JEWISH SERVICES.

songs, called psalms, suitable for chanting in the worship of God. David had written dozens of psalms himself. Every emotion, every thought was conveyed to God. His psalms asked for God's help, praised God, showed sorrow, and celebrated how great God was.

In the years ahead, David found Jonathan's only living descendant, a crippled young man named Mephibosheth. David took him into his palace and treated him like one of his own sons. David's family was very large.

His armies conquered more neighboring nations, including the Moabites and the Arameans. His armies fought Zobah, Hamath, the Amalekites, the Edomites, and the Ammonites. His army ventured far north to subdue the Syrians.

After ten years in Jerusalem, it seemed to David that he had everything. Then one spring evening, he looked down over the city from his palace roof and saw a woman bathing. She was so

HIS ARMIES FOUGHT ZOBAH, HAMATH, AND THE ARAMEANS.

beautiful he was overcome with desire for her. He wanted her for his wife. He sent a servant to find out who she was.

"She is Bathsheba, the wife of Uriah," said the servant when he returned.

"Bathsheba," murmured David.

Although he was forty-seven years old and had many wives, David could scarcely think straight because he was so taken with this woman. He had come to expect his every wish to be satisfied. He summoned Bathsheba. When he met her, he was smitten by her beauty.

David decided he was going to marry Bathsheba. David knew Uriah was an officer in his army. In fact Uriah was with Joab, who was currently leading the fighting against the Ammonites at their main city of Rabbah. Rabbah was about twenty miles east of the River Jordan. Located on the heavily traveled trade route called the King's Highway, Rabbah was considered quite a prize.

HE WAS SMITTEN BY HER BEAUTY.

DAVID

David was intensely interested in the outcome of the fighting. But now he schemed against his own officer: Uriah!

David sent a message to Joab:

*Put Uriah in the front line where the fighting is fiercest. Then withdraw from him so he will be struck down and die.**

Then David sat back and waited. Several days later a messenger arrived from the front lines.

*2 Samuel 11:15

A MESSENGER ARRIVED FROM THE FRONT LINES.

"SOME OF YOUR MEN DIED. . ."

10

The messenger from Rabbah stood at attention before David. "Ammonites came out against us from the city gate—"

"Yes, yes, go on!" David sputtered impatiently.

"But we drove them back—"

"Yes, go on!"

"Then archers shot arrows at us—"

"Go on!"

"Some of your men died—"

David rose menacingly. "Finish your report!"

DAVID

"Moreover, your servant Uriah is dead."

David could barely keep from rejoicing. "Tell Joab that these losses must not upset him. One man dies in battle as well as another. Press the attack. Destroy Rabbah!"

When the messenger departed, David collapsed in his throne. The deed was done. Bathsheba was his. All that separated her from David was her period of mourning for her dead husband. Then David would bring her into the palace as his wife!

From the palace he observed people rushing into Bathsheba's house. Soon loud wailing was heard. Because Uriah was wealthy, his family hired additional mourners to wail and chant their grief. Even musicians were hired to play heart-rending dirges on their flutes. All the while David waited impatiently in the palace.

Even when Joab and David's army returned in triumph after leaving Rabbah in ruins, David was distracted by his wait. Finally, after several weeks, Bathsheba was brought into the palace. David and

SOON LOUD WAILING WAS HEARD.

Bathsheba loved each other very much.

One day Nathan, David's main prophet, asked for an audience. David agreed, somewhat surprised that Nathan insisted they meet privately. Nathan told him a story:

There were two men in a certain town, one rich and the other poor. The rich man had a very large number of sheep and cattle, but the poor man had nothing except one little ewe lamb he had bought. He raised it, and it grew up with him and his children. It shared his food, drank from his cup and even slept in his arms. It was like a daughter to him.

Now a traveler came to the rich man, but the rich man refrained from taking one of his own sheep or cattle to prepare a meal for the traveler who had come to him. Instead, he took the ewe lamb that belonged to the poor man and

NATHAN TOLD HIM A STORY.

DAVID

*prepared it for the one who had come to him.**

David exploded in anger. "What? As surely as Almighty God is alive that rich man should die!"

Nathan looked David straight in the eye. "You, sir, are that rich man."

"Me?"

"You have many wives, yet you took the one wife of Uriah by having him killed by the sword of the Ammonites. For that great sin your family will endure disaster after disaster."

David retreated to a private room, reeling. What had he done? By his sin he had brought God's wrath against his own family! Always the poet he composed a song of sorrow which started with a confession:

Have mercy on me, O God,
according to your unfailing love;

---

*2 Samuel 12:1–4

WHAT HAD HE DONE?

DAVID

according to your great compassion
blot out my transgressions.
Wash away all my iniquity
and cleanse me from my sin.

For I know my transgressions,
*and my sin is always before me.**

Near the end of his sad song, David begged
for forgiveness:

Create in me a pure heart, O God,
and renew a steadfast spirit within me.
Do not cast me from your presence
or take your Holy Spirit from me.
Restore to me the joy of your salvation
and grant me a willing spirit, to sustain me.
Then I will teach transgressors your ways,
and sinners will turn back to you.

---

*Psalm 51:1–3

"CREATE IN ME A PURE HEART, O GOD."

DAVID

Save me from bloodguilt, O God,
the God who saves me, and my tongue
will sing of your righteousness.*

David had confessed his sin. He had repented. But that did not relieve him of God's punishment. The first disaster soon struck. Bathsheba gave birth to a son, but the baby got sick. David pleaded with God to let the boy live.

The baby died.

"I will go to him, but he will not return to me," David said sadly about his dead son.

David meant that he would join his son in eternity. David loved God, and God loved him in spite of his sinfulness. A song one of his priests had composed expressed his feeling:

But God will redeem my life from the grave;
he will surely take me to himself.†

---

*Psalm 51:10–14

†Psalm 49:15

THE BABY DIED.

But David had little time to mourn. Never had his kingdom made so many demands on him. His inner circle included Ahithophel and Hushai, his counselors; Jehoshaphat and Sheva, his recorders; Nathan, his prophet; and Abiathar and Jairite, his personal priests.

Constantly he agonized over who to assign to which jobs. Of course Joab, his highest general, ran his large royal army, but David approved of every assignment, every promotion. Hashabiah and Zadok administered a very complex organization of priests and musicians in the tabernacle. Each of the twelve Jewish tribes also had to have a leader who was loyal to the king. David assigned his own tribe of Judah to his brother Elihu, and gave the tribe of Simeon to his son Shephatiah.

The royal property required much oversight because David was now the wealthiest of the wealthy. He had faithful managers in charge of the storehouses, the field workers, the vineyards, the orchards, the olive presses, the stables of donkeys

HE HAD FAITHFUL MANAGERS IN CHARGE.

and camels, and the vast herds of cattle, sheep, and goats. But because of Nathan's warning, David worried over what disaster would next strike his family.

He soon found out.

DAVID WORRIED OVER WHAT DISASTER WOULD STRIKE NEXT.

TAMAR'S EYES WERE RED FROM WEEPING.

11

Amnon, David and Ahinoam's son, was a young man. One day Amnon pretended to be sick. He stayed in his bedroom and asked David to send Tamar to visit him. She was such a comforting person.

Tamar was Amnon's half-sister. She was the daughter of David and Maacah. So David sent Tamar to visit Amnon.

Later, Tamar's brother Absalom saw her. He was shocked. Tamar's eyes were red from weeping.

She had put ashes on her head and torn her elegant robe.

"What has happened?" gasped Absalom. "Did Amnon attack you?"

Tears poured down Tamar's face.

"Don't worry, my sister," Absalom said. "Come live in my house. I will protect you."

When David learned what had happened, he was very angry. But he did not punish Amnon for attacking his sister. This made Absalom very angry. He loved his sister and thought Amnon should pay for attacking her. He waited for a chance to get even with Amnon.

Two years later, all of David's sons went to the annual sheep shearing in late spring. Absalom was in charge. David had thousands of sheep, and when the shearing was finished the workers celebrated. But the news David got from the shearing was not joyous. While all the sons were enjoying the party, Absalom had his servants kill Amnon!

"It was because Amnon attacked his sister,

DAVID'S SONS WENT TO THE SHEEP SHEARING.

Tamar," said David's nephew Jonadab.

Absalom was glad that he had paid back Amnon for what he had done. But Absalom was afraid that he would now be punished. So Absalom ran away to the nation of Geshur, located east of the Sea of Galilee. Geshur welcomed him because his mother, Maacah, was the daughter of one of its kings.

David mourned the loss of both of his sons. Amnon was dead, and Absalom might as well have been dead. He was living far away, and David could not forgive him. It was three years before Joab, David's nephew and head general, persuaded David to let Absalom return to the palace.

"After all, didn't Amnon attack Absalom's sister, Tamar?" Joab reminded the king. "Because of that attack, Tamar has never married or had children."

"Go get him then," agreed David. "But I won't see him."

DAVID MOURNED THE DEATH OF HIS SONS.

So Absalom returned. Most people did not blame him for his crime. Besides, Absalom was one of the most handsome men in the kingdom. His glossy, black hair was full and long like the magnificent mane of a lion. Of all the Jews, only Absalom drove a chariot attended by fifty footmen. The people were thrilled with his flair for the colorful. After Absalom had been back in Jerusalem for two years, David finally forgave him.

But rumors soon reached David that Absalom was endearing himself to all the visiting dignitaries by entertaining them and promising them favors with the king. There was no doubt that Absalom was popular—but at what price? And what was he planning to do with that popularity?

Several years later Absalom told David, "I wish to go to Hebron and worship God."

"Go in peace," said David.

David was now nearly sixty years old. He thought that Absalom's trip was unusual because the young man was not known for loving God and

ABSALOM DROVE A CHARIOT.

going to services. Moreover, Absalom had invited two hundred of the most important Jews in Israel to go with him. Later, David learned his chief counselor Ahithophel was also at Hebron. Yes, the gathering seemed most unusual.

One day a soldier burst in. "I come from Hebron. Absalom has declared himself king of all the Jews!"

David quickly assessed his situation. Absalom had engineered a very successful rebellion. Although Joab remained faithful to David, most of the army was under Absalom's control. No doubt he was marching on Jerusalem that very moment.

"We must flee Jerusalem!" David heard himself saying.

Imagine, after ruling for so many years he was fleeing his own City of David! He still possessed an army of several thousand soldiers including his royal guard. But he would not be trapped within the city and have his loyal followers starved by Absalom. Besides, David was the master of

A SOLDIER BURST IN.

surviving in the wilderness.

With his army and his household, he marched down from his great walled city into the Kidron Valley east of Jerusalem. Then David's party marched up the Mount of Olives with its rich orchards. There David told the priests Zadok and Abiathar that they must go back to Jerusalem and remain at the tabernacle to protect the Ark of the Covenant.

Then David instructed his loyal counselor Hushai, "You must go back, too. Pledge your allegiance to Absalom. But foil his plans any way you can. And send information to me in the wilderness through the two sons of Zadok and Abiathar. I will await them at the River Jordan."

With those final instructions, David and his followers marched off into the wilderness. At first they traveled the well-used road to Jericho. Few roads were steeper. The travelers left Jerusalem in the cool highlands and descended to Jericho in blistering lowlands. On the way, David's entourage

DAVID'S ARMY MARCHED UP THE MOUNT OF OLIVES.

passed a man named Shimei. Shimei was one of the few survivors of the house of King Saul.

"Curse you, King David!" screamed Shimei. "God has repaid you for all the blood on your hands!"

Abishai, Joab's brother and David's nephew, growled, "Let me go kill that dog."

"Leave him alone," snapped David. "If my own son Absalom is trying to kill me, why are you concerned with this relative of King Saul?"

Then David led his party off the main road and down a ravine to the River Jordan. There they waited for the two sons of the priests to come. Days passed before the two young men showed up. Breathlessly they told David that Absalom wanted to set out for David immediately but that Hushai had advised him to build a huge force first. Now David had time to cross the River Jordan and hide in the eastern mountains.

"CURSE YOU, KING DAVID!"

THEY ATE HEARTILY.

12

So David crossed the River Jordan and marched on to the Ammonite city of Mahanaim. Although David had long fought the Ammonites, they respected him. He was welcome. The tired travelers were furnished bedding and utensils. They ate heartily of bread, beans, lentils, cheese, and honey.

"We must prepare to battle Absalom's army," David said to Joab and two other commanders. "We will divide the forces into three groups. I will march with you."

"No!" objected Joab. "You are worth ten thousand of us. If Absalom's troops recognize you, they will never stop until they kill you."

"I won't go then, but please spare my son Absalom," he pleaded.

So David waited in the city, getting reports of armies moving here and there. Soon it became clear that Joab—a great general—had lured Absalom's army into the forests north of Mahanaim. Absalom's superior numbers did him no good at all. His men scattered through the forest, lost and bewildered. Joab's more disciplined troops cut them down. Many deserted Absalom's army.

David waited within the walls of Mahanaim. Soon he learned that Absalom's army had been routed. But what of Absalom? He was killed.

David screamed, "Oh my son Absalom! My son, my son Absalom! If only I had died instead of you!"

David felt enormous guilt over Absalom. If he had handled the situation with Tamar the way

JOAB LURED ABSALOM'S ARMY INTO THE FORESTS.

a father should have, Absalom would not have been tempted to commit murder and go into exile. Then David had ignored his son for many years. Who knew how bitter the experience had made Absalom?

The details of Absalom's death depressed David even more. Absalom's long, flowing hair had gotten tangled in a tree. Helpless, he had been speared many times by David's army. Joab threw the first spear.

David railed, "Didn't I tell Joab and his army not to kill Absalom?"

But Joab was just as angry. He went to talk to King David. "It seems you love those who hate you and hate those who love you," he said. "You would be pleased if Absalom were alive today and all of us were dead!"

Although David was sick at heart and wanted to kill Joab, he didn't. Joab was right in being angry with him. Joab and his other loyal followers had saved his kingdom. Besides, David felt his

JOAB THREW THE FIRST SPEAR.

own sin had created problems for Absalom. Nathan had warned David long ago that God would forgive him but that David would still be punished.

Still, David returned to Jerusalem in triumph. But age slowed him more and more. Once, perhaps feeling guilty because he sat out the great battle in the forests north of Mahanaim, David joined a skirmish with the Philistines to the west. During the battle the weight of his armor made him so tired that he collapsed. His nephew Abishai struck down one of the giants of Gath just as he bore down on David.

"Never again!" swore David's commanders. They tried to soften their anger by saying, "We will not let the lamp of Israel be extinguished."

David's commanders were right. He must rule. For his ability to run the kingdom remained strong. So did his creative ability as Israel's singer of songs. David still composed psalms:

THE WEIGHT OF THE ARMOR MADE HIM SO TIRED THAT HE COLLAPSED.

DAVID

*The LORD is my rock, my fortress and
my deliverer; my God is my rock, in
whom I take refuge. He is my shield
and the horn of my salvation, my
stronghold.*

*I call to the LORD, who is worthy of
praise, and I am saved from my
enemies.**

David wrote down the names of his greatest
warriors, whom he called his mighty men. Among
the thirty-seven men listed was Uriah. How terrible David felt as he wrote that name. He had murdered one of his own mighty men! He shuddered.
But it seemed as he approached seventy years of
age that he could not stop shuddering. Would he
be able to control another rebellious son? He soon
found out.

---

*Psalm 18:2–3

DAVID WROTE DOWN THE NAMES OF HIS GREATEST WARRIORS.

This time it was Adonijah, David and Haggith's son, who plotted to become king. He was pulling people away from David, including Joab and Abiathar. Perhaps these two loyal followers felt David was now too feeble to govern. Would Adonijah succeed at what Absalom had failed to do?

But Bathsheba knew what few people knew. "Did you not swear to me," she asked David, "that our son Solomon would inherit your throne?"

"That was commanded not by me but by God," answered David. "My prophet Nathan told me." David also knew that Solomon would build the great temple of stone that God would not allow him to build.

At that moment Nathan angrily entered. "Have you told Adonijah he is to inherit the throne? He is celebrating already."

David had reigned for forty years. He realized he could no longer cling to the throne. He gave his last commands, "Have Zadok the high priest anoint

DAVID HAD REIGNED FOR FORTY YEARS.

Solomon king of Israel immediately. Blow the trumpets and shout, 'Long live King Solomon!' "

With the announcement that twenty-one-year-old Solomon was king, there was great jubilation. Adonijah's ambition evaporated. His allies deserted him. But Solomon spared his brother's life after warning him to go home and cause no trouble. Knowing Adonijah as he did, David doubted the man could keep out of trouble.

At seventy, David's health failed rapidly. He was an old ram, but God would shepherd him to the end. He sang one of his songs that said exactly what was in his heart and soul:

The LORD is my shepherd, I shall not be
in want.
He makes me lie down in green pastures,
he leads me beside quiet waters,
he restores my soul.
He guides me in paths of righteousness
for his name's sake.

"LONG LIVE KING SOLOMON!"

DAVID

*Even though I walk through the valley of
    the shadow of death,
I will fear no evil, for you are with me; your
    rod and your staff, they comfort me.
You prepare a table before me in the
    presence of my enemies.
You anoint my head with oil;
    my cup overflows.
Surely goodness and love will follow me
    all the days of my life, and I will dwell
    in the house of the LORD forever.**

"I am about to go the way of all flesh," David told Solomon. "Be strong, show yourself a man, and obey God. Walk in His ways, and keep His commandments as written in the Law of Moses. Some day one of our descendants will be Messiah of Israel."

One thousand years later, one of David's descendants was born in Bethlehem. He was Jesus of Nazareth, the Messiah, the Son of God!

---

*Psalm 23

HE WAS JESUS OF NAZARETH, THE SON OF GOD!

AWESOME BOOKS FOR KIDS!

The Young Reader's Christian Library
Action, Adventure, and Fun Reading!

This series for young readers ages 8 to 12 is action-packed, fast-paced, and Christ-centered! With exciting illustrations on every other page following the text, these books are hard for kids to put down! Over 100 illustrations per book. All books are paperbound. The unique size (4 ⅛" x 5 ⅜") makes these books easy to take anywhere!

A Great Selection to Satisfy All Kids!

Abraham Lincoln	Heidi	Pocahontas
Ben-Hur	Hudson Taylor	Pollyanna
Billy Graham	In His Steps	Prudence of Plymouth
Billy Sunday	Jesus	Plantation
Christopher	Jim Elliot	Robinson Crusoe
Columbus	Joseph	Roger Williams
Corrie ten Boom	Little Women	Ruth
Daniel	Lydia	Samuel Morris
David Brainerd	Miriam	The Swiss Family
David Livingstone	Moses	Robinson
Deborah	Paul	Thunder in the
Elijah	Peter	Valley
Esther	The Pilgrim's	Wagons West
Florence Nightingale	Progress	